Randall Cooke Hall

Some Elements of Hebrew Grammar

Randall Cooke Hall

Some Elements of Hebrew Grammar

ISBN/EAN: 9783337317416

Printed in Europe, USA, Canada, Australia, Japan

Cover: Foto ©Paul-Georg Meister /pixelio.de

More available books at **www.hansebooks.com**

SOME ELEMENTS

OF

HEBREW GRAMMAR.

BY THE

REV. RANDALL C. HALL, D.D.,

"CLEMENT C. MOORE" PROFESSOR OF THE HEBREW AND GREEK
LANGUAGES IN THE GENERAL THEOLOGICAL SEMINARY.

THIRD EDITION.

PUBLISHED BY THE AUTHOR

FOR THE USE OF HIS CLASSES.

NEW YORK, 1888.

SYLLABLES.

§ 1. Every syllable must begin with a consonant, except that a word may begin with וֹ.

The syllable may end—

(*a*) With a vowel. Such a syllable is called pure, or open, or simple.

(*b*) With a consonant, or possibly at the end of a word with two consonants. Such a syllable is called mixed or closed.

§ 2. A syllable is called *intermediate* (also half open or half closed) when it is, strictly speaking, neither pure nor mixed, but wavers between these two states.

The consonant, frequently a guttural, which tends to close it, tends also to begin the next syllable, and belongs, therefore, in a measure to the two syllables, *e. g.*, the first syllable in הָעֵת֑,

יַ֫עֲמֹד ,יַעֲמֹד֙ ,קָדָשִׁים֙, qŏ‿dhā-shīm', מַלְכֵי֫ mă‿l'khēy', קְלָלַת qĭ‿l'láth, קְטָלִי֫ qĭ‿t'lī' (fem. of קְטֹל q'tōl), the first two syllables of יַעֲמֹד֫וּ

Intermediate syllables thus wavering between the natures of pure and mixed, some look like pure syllables, others like mixed, and in some cases grammarians disagree as to their classification.

§ 3. The nature of the syllable depends on the development of the word to which it belongs. Thus, in the qal imperative קְטֹל the ט is joined to ל in forming a syllable. In forming from this the feminine, the addition of the termination ־י breaks up the mixed syllable, and removes its vowel—thus, קְטְלִי. The ט then tends to join ק in forming a new syllable קְטְלִי (for the first vowel see § 41); but it tends also to retain its old union with ל in forming a syllable, as is shown by the vocal sh'va under it, qĭ‿t'lī'. Thus the first syllable is intermediate, and the vocal sh'va echoes the dropped vowel.

§ 4. Hence, conversely, the analysis of a word is often aided by knowing the nature of a syllable, and thus its etymology is determined. Thus if אָרְבָּם (Hos. vii. 6) were an infinitive, the first syllable would be intermediate, which it cannot be, as shown by the daghesh in בּ, § 28. For the development of the infinitive see § 106.

§ 5. An asyllabic addition is an affix or suffix which in itself is not a syllable—e. g., ־ִים, ־ֶ, ־וֹ, ־ָה, ־ָם, ־ֵם, ־וֹ.

AFFIXES AND SUFFIXES.

§ 6. Affixes and suffixes are additions to the ends of words.

The suffixes and some of the affixes are fragments of pronouns.

The affixes show the gender, number, and person of words which they terminate.

The suffixes represent the oblique cases of pronouns, and have retained even in Hebrew more of their identity and independence than the affixes, but in Latin and Greek they are expressed by separate words. In קְטַלּוּנִי the וּ is an affix, and the נִי a suffix. In סוּסָתוֹ ת֒ is an affix, and וֹ a suffix.

ACCENT.

---

§ 7. Accents may or may not mark the tone. An accent is called *prepositive* when it is always on the first letter of a word, without regard to the tone. An accent is called *postpositive* when it is always on the last letter of a word, without regard to the tone.

Those accents which mark the tone are either above or below the first consonant of the tone syllable. If below, they are to the left of any vowel point which may be under the consonant. Methegh likewise is attached to the first consonant of its syllable and to the left of any vowel point which may be under the consonant.

In this manual the tone is marked *over* the word by an oblique stroke, and is thus distinguished from methegh.

TONE.

§ 8. When the tone is on the ultimate, a word is called milra (from below); when on the penult, it is called milel (from above).

(*a*) The tone is never further back than the penult—*i. e.*, two syllables.

(*b*) Vocal sh'va is a vowel sound, and with its consonant counts half a syllable in the laws of accentuation. [Hence a sh'va after the tone is usually silent. But in cases of a paragogic vowel, *e. g.*, הַ local and י , Ps. ciii. 3, and when a conjunctive recedes before a disjunctive, the tone may stand back, *e. g.*, to the right of vocal sh'va; in other words, be two and a half syllables back.]

(*c*) The tone is called *recessive* when it is as far back as rules permit. This position is called *the tone limit*.

§ 9. No tone rests on

(*a*) A letter with sh'va, or with a vowel which has arisen from compound sh'va, cf. § 10 (*c*).

(*b*) A helping vowel (especially of a segholate) unless the word be a monosyllable, *e. g.*, סֻוּסֵךְ.

(*c*) ה paragogic of nouns, particularly ה local. [Other things being equal, the tone usually avoids a paragogic vowel. But י paragogic of nouns takes tone, Ps. cxiii.]

Remark. —§ 9 takes precedence when conflicting with other rules, *e. g.*, with §§ 11 and 16, מֶ֫לֶךְ, קְטָ֫לַת

§ 10. A long vowel cannot stand in a mixed syllable, nor a short vowel in a pure syllable, without tone, or, as in some cases, methegh.

(*a*) If, therefore, in developing a word a long vowel is left beyond the tone limit in a mixed syllable, it must be shortened; or if a short vowel is left in a pure syllable beyond the tone limit, it must be lengthened, or else daghesh forte must be inserted in the following consonant to preserve the vowel short, hence called daghesh forte conservative.

(1) A change of quantity often involves a change of quality, particularly in the case of the last four vowels—e and i, o and u, cf. § 33.

(*b*) The tone tends to lengthen the short vowel of a pure syllable, and in some cases of a mixed ultimate.

(*c*) The vowel of an intermediate syllable is short and unaccented.

§ 11. Words in their uninflected state usually take tone on the ultimate.

6

Position of Tone on Verbs.

§ 12. The vowel of the second radical takes the tone when rules permit.

§ 13. In the preterite 1st and 2d masculine singular with vav conversive, the tone is on the ultimate (to distinguish from the same forms with vav conjunctive), except sometimes when the penult is pure, and also when a conjunctive recedes before a disjunctive.

§ 14. The future 2d and 3d singular with vav conversive take tone on the penult, if the penult is pure and the ultimate mixed.

Remark.—§§ 13 and 14 often fail to affect a pause accent.

§ 15. Some apocopated futures being properly segholates, follow the rule for segholates. See § 9 (b).

Tone as Affected by Affixes and Suffixes.

§ 16. An asyllabic addition to a *noun* takes tone (also the initial vowel of יִ and יָךְ).

§ 17. An asyllabic addition to a *verb*—
(a) If affix, does not affect the tone unless other rules require.
(b) If suffix, draws the tone forward one syllable.

§ 18. The addition of a pure syllable requires recessive [§ 8 (c)] tone.

§ 19. The addition of a mixed syllable takes tone on itself.

§ 20. Participles, infinitives, adjectives, and prepositions, are accented as nouns. Also participles and adjectives are inflected as nouns.

§ 21. The shifting of the tone towards the end of a word tends to the shortening and dropping of vowels at the beginning, especially when such shifting is due to an addition at the end.

§ 22. In pause there is a tendency to shift the tone from the ultimate to the penult.

§ 23. A pause accent changes into seghol a simple sh'va before the suffix ךָ and in triliteral syllables, and lengthens a short vowel.

§ 24. A conjunctive accent joins the word on which it stands more or less closely to what follows. A disjunctive separates it more or less from what follows.

METHEGH.

§ 25. (*a*) A syllable the second or fourth before the tone usually takes methegh, but a mixed syllable may fail to receive it or shift it to an antecedent pure syllable.

(*b*) A pure syllable takes methegh if followed by a sh'va.

(*c*) An intermediate syllable taks methegh also if followed by a compound sh'va, or by a vowel which has arisen from a compound sh'va, and frequently also if followed by a simple sh'va.

8

PRACTICAL USE OF METHEGH.

§ 26. We see, therefore, that such a word as qā-t'lāh *must* take methegh, thus—קָֽמְלָֽה׃

But qŏ‿t'lāh or even qŏt-lāh, with like vowel signs, *might* take methegh, though as a matter of fact this would be unusual.

Hence in such a form as קָמְלָֽה the absence of methegh proves the first syllable either mixed or intermediate [for, if simple, being followed by sh'va, it would take methegh by § 25 (*b*)], and, therefore, kamets short by § 30.

But the presence of methegh would not prove the first syllable pure or kamets long, though there would be a strong presumption in favor of these inferences. In such a case the only sure guide is the development of the word.

§ 27. In like manner we see that in such a form as יִרְאֽוּ ("they shall see") the absence of methegh proves that the first syllable is either mixed or intermediate [for, if pure, being followed by a sh'va, it would take methegh by § 25 (*b*)] and, therefore, chī-req, short by § 30. On the other hand, in יִרְאֽוּ we should have reason to suspect the first syllable to be pure, and, therefore, the meaning to be "they shall fear." In the manner are distinguished יִשְׁנֽוּ, "they shall repeat," and יִֽשְׁנֽוּ, "they shall sleep."

DAGHESH LENE.

§ 28. B'ghadh k'phath letters take daghesh lene when not preceded by a vowel sound in close connection.

(*a*) Also other consonants preceded by a vowelless guttural in the same word take daghesh lene in some editions.

(*b*) Final kā, kem, and ken never take daghesh lene. From this we infer that a preceding sh'va is vocal.

MAPPIQ AND RAPHE.

§ 29. Daghesh lene, daghesh forte, and mappiq have a common design—viz., to indicate the strong sound of a letter.

Map-piq (bringing out or uttering) in final ה shows that it is a consonant, and not a quiescent.

Rā-phé (weak) denotes the opposite of daghesh lene, daghesh forte, or mappiq, as the case may be.

VOWELS.

§ 30. The vowels i and u and the sign ָ (qamets) are short in unaccented mixed, or in intermediate syllables. Otherwise they are long.

These are called doubtful signs, to which we we may add sh'va simple.

(*a*) A defective chīreq is frequently long, but a full one is rarely short.

§ 31. To determine the length of the doubtful vowel in such a form as קָטְלוֹ. Here it is short because in an unaccented mixed, or in an intermediate syllable.

We know that the syllable is either mixed or intermediate, for if pure it would take methegh by § 25 (*b*).

§ 32. The sign ָ (qamets), if followed by a short "o" sound (either ֹ or ׃) is itself also very likely to be short "o," and must be, if sympathetic.

(*a*) A vowel which conforms with another or with which another conforms is called "sympathetic" in this manual.

§ 33. The pure vowels are
The diphthongal vowels are

$$a \diagdown \quad \diagup i \qquad \diagup u$$
$$\diagdown e \diagup \diagdown o \diagup$$

This diagram means that e is formed by combining a and i; o is formed by combining a and u.

(*a*) A change of quantity often involves a change of quality, more particularly in the case of the last four vowels—e and i, o and u.

(*b*) In *accented* syllables, before a double consonant or before two consonants, diphthongal are preferred to the pure vowels i and u (and sometimes even e is changed to a, *e. g.*, הׇקְטַלְתׇּ, קְטַלְתׇּ, יָסַב from יְסֵב.

(*c*) In unaccented syllables before a doubled consonant, the pure vowels i and u are preferred to the diphthongal e and o.

§ 34. An impure vowel is one in which a vowel letter quiesces, or after which a vowel letter has dropped out, or which contains the force of a daghesh.

§ 35. A vowel letter is called otiant when it is not sounded and yet has no vowel in which to quiesce.

§ 36. The gutturals being closely akin to the "a" sound, have a strong preference for this vowel, especially before them.

§ 37. A final vowelless guttural not preceded by an "a" sound takes pattach furtive (also a vowelless guttural followed by a final vowelless consonant takes pattach furtive).

§ 38. A guttural, especially if unaccented, between two "a" sounds will often cause one of them, more frequently the former, to become seghol (in order to give distinctness to the enunciation of the guttural).

(*a*) Before הַ and עַ (ā) unaccented and before הָ (ā) (not necessarily a pure syllable), and הָ֬, the article is pointed with seghol, and in general a pattach is chánged to seghol.

§ 39. A guttural prefers a compound to a simple sh'va, and in particular ־ֲ, unless there is a reason for preferring some other compound sh'va. Of course such a reason exists when the sh'va should conform with an " e " or an " o " sound.

(*a*) A simple sh'va under a guttural is always silent.

§ 40. An initial letter with sh'va when immediately before the tone has preference for a pretonic vowel, especially qamets.

§ 41. When, in consequence of changes, two vocal sh'vas concur, for the first a short vowel is substituted (which may be called an auxiliary vowel).

1. If (*a*) both be simple [or (*b*) the first an unsympathetic compound sh'va], i is substituted [(*c*) unless a reason exists for preferring a, or e, or o.]

2. If the second be a compound sh'va the previous syllable conforms, *i. e.*, takes the homogeneous vowel.

3. If the first be (*a*) a characteristic or (*b*) a sympathetic compound sh'va, the chateph is suppressed (*e. g.*, -ֱ: becomes -).

Examples.—Of 1 (*a*): קְטְלִי becomes קָטְלִי, בְּפְרִי becomes בָּפְרִי.

Of 1 (*b*): עֲמְדִי becomes עִמְדִי.

Of 1 (*c*): מְלְכֵי becomes מַלְכֵי, because pattach was its primitive vowel; also הֲמְעַט becomes הַמְעַט, because the "a" sound characterizes ה interrogative; cf. 3 (*a*) of the above rule.

Of 2: יַעֲמֹד becomes יַעֲמֹד, נִדְחֲךָ becomes נִדַּחֲךָ, Deut. xxx. 4.

Of 3 (*a*): הֲמְעַט becomes הַמְעַט; cf. 1 (*c*) above.

Of 3 (*b*): תַּעֲמְדִי becomes תַּעַמְדִי, אֱהֶבוּ becomes אֶהֱבוּ.

§ 42. When two simple sh'vas concur at the beginning of a word, chireq is commonly substituted for the first. [It will be observed that this rule is a repetition of § 41, 1 (*a*).]

43. A final vowelless consonant does not take sh'va, but if preceded by another vowelless consonant they both take sh'va.

MAQQEPH.

44. Maqqeph removes the tone from the ˙preceding word. If thereby a long vowel is left in a mixed syllable, being toneless, it must be shortened by § 10.

NOUNS.

45. Before the plural terminations and sometimes before the dual, segholates take pretonic qamets and drop their first vowel.

46. Segholates revert to their primitive form—
    (*a*) in the singular before all suffixes;
    (*b*) before the termination ‎הָ;
    (*c*) in the construct dual and plural;
    (*d*) usually in the dual absolute.
    Remark 1.—This rule takes precedence when conflicting with other rules, except § 49 Remark.
    Remark 2.—(*c*) is used in the application of § 41, 1, ˙ the construct of the plural and sometimes of the dual being formed from the absolute by applying § 49 (*b*).

47. Before the plural and dual terminations, and before the feminine termination ‎הָ, the following changes take place—
    (*a*) In the ultimate, tsere is rejected, except in a monosyllable, or in a syllable preceded by qamets.

(*b*) In the penult, qamets and tsere are rejected, unless in the resulting form they remain pretonic.

Remark 1.—Before the dual termination, the feminine singular reverts to its primitive termination ן.

In all other cases the above terminations are added to the absolute singular masculine, which is assumed, if necessary.

Remark 2.—By the ultimate and penult in the above rule are meant, of course, the ultimate and penult of the noun before the addition in question is made.

§ 48. The ending ה ֶ of nouns is dropped before additions.

Remark.—This rule takes precedence when conflicting with other rules.

CONSTRUCT STATE.

§ 49. The construct state of each number is formed from its respective absolute.

(*a*) In a mixed final syllable, qamets is shortened to pattach, and so is tsere if preceded by qamets.

(*b*) Qamets and tsere before the tone are rejected.

Remark.—Sh'va is vocal in the construct plural and dual when arising from dropping a pretonic vowel.

§ 50. Medi l ן frequently quiesces in cholem, and medial י in tsere in the construct and before additions.

Before Suffixes.

51. Before the grave suffixes (kem, ken, hem, and hen), all nouns take construct state.

52. Before light suffixes, feminine nouns, singular and plural, take construct state.

53. Before light suffixes, masculine nouns, singular and plural, take the same form as before the absolute plural termination.

54. Before light suffixes, dual nouns take the same form as before the absolute dual termination.
Remark.—In applying §§ 52 and 53, a noun is treated as masculine unless it has a distinctively feminine termination.

Verbs.

55. If the future qal is middle a, the imperative is middle a.
[(a) The imperative of each species is from the primitive form of its respective future by dropping the prefix of the future, and the future is from the infinitive construct by prefixing ׳ and

contracting, if necessary; cf. the pointing of the excluded article.

56. Verbs ayin guttural, lamedh guttural, and lamedh aleph have middle a in the future and imperative qal.

57. In verbs lamedh guttural, tsere before the guttural is changed to pattach, except in the infinitive absolute, and participle, and in pause.

§ 58. In verbs pe nun—

(*a*) When the nun is pointed with silent sh'va, the nun is usually dropped, and the next letter takes daghesh to compensate.

(*b*) The nun of the qal imperative is usually dropped if middle a, very seldom if middle o.

(*c*) Nun is dropped in qal infinitive construct of but few verbs, and then the infinitive takes the feminine termination ת, and is of segholate formation.

§ 59. In verbs ayin ayin, the second radical frequently disappears by way of contraction, and its vowel is given to the first.

§ 60. In verbs ayin vav and ayin yodh, the middle radical gives its vowel to the first, and then either

(*a*) disappears, or

(*b*) unites with this vowel to form a diphthongal vowel, or

(*c*) quiesces in it after changing it to the vowel most akin to the second radical (the semi-vowel vav being most nearly akin to ū, and yodh to ī).

§ 61. In verbs ayin ayin and ayin vav the preformative usually takes a long vowel in the future qal, preterite niphal, and throughout hiphil and hophal (when not affected by the shifting of the tone; but when so affected the vowel is dropped, if mutable).

Remark.—This rule is not fundamental, but serves to illustrate the application of other rules, *e. g.*, of §§ 10 and 40.

62. In verbs ayin ayin, before an affix beginning with a nun or tav, an epenthetic vowel is added—viz., וֹ in the preterite, וֹ in the future and imperative.

(a) This usually occurs also in the future qal and preterites niphal and hiphil of verbs ayin vav.

63. 1. In verbs pe yodh, properly pe vav, there are two subdivisions in qal future, imperative, and infinitive construct.

(u) In the first subdivision, the yodh of the root is dropped in these parts; the preformative of the future has tsere, and the infinitive construct has the ending ת, and is of segholate formation.

(b) In the second subdivision, the yodh of the root is retained in these parts, the future has a middle a, and its preformative has chireq.

2. The vav is restored in niphal, hiphil, and hophal.

64. 1. In verbs lamedh he, before an affix beginning with nun or tav, the original וֹ remains, but is quiescent. In the future and imperative it quiesces in seghol; in the preterite qal, in chireq; in the preterites pual and hophal, in tsere; in the preterites of the other species, in chireq or tsere.

2. Before an affix beginning with a vowel and before a suffix, the last radical and the preceding vowel usually fall away, as also ה ֶ of nouns drops out before additions, cf. § 48.

65. 1. The jussive of a future whose last vowel is i or u is obtained by a change to the corresponding diphthongal vowel.

2. The jussive is not used with additions at the end.

§ 66. By examining the verb qatal, it is seen that the addition of a vowel as affix (except in hiphil) causes the middle radical to lose its vowel. This analogy is not followed when involving the loss of a radical.

(a) But if this vowel is capable of taking the tone, a pause accent preserves it, and lengthens it, if short.

§ 67. Before additions, primitive forms are often restored. In particular, before suffixes the primitive forms of verbs are restored.

Syntax.

§ 68. כֹּל indefinite in a negative sentence makes the negation universal.

§ 69. As regards the order of subject and predicate (e. g., in such a sentence as—The boy is good) the general rule is that the more emphatic word precedes. Hence a predicate adjective (because usually regarded as more emphatic than the subject) usually precedes the subject.

§ 70. A *qualifying* adjective follows its noun, and takes the article, if the noun is definite.

§ 71. The force of the infinitive construct, imperative, and participle is often carried on by the future or preterite.

Q'RI AND K'THIBH.

§ 72. Hebrew manuscripts were originally written with consonants only, without any Massoretic points. This writing was called the k'thibh, *i. e.*, written. Another name for it is the Text. In most cases the text is pronounced with the Massoretic points attached to it. The Massoretic points are the vowels, daghesh forte, daghesh lene, the diacritical point, mappiq, and raphe.

When the Massorites thought an emendation necessary, as they did not dare to disturb the text, they usually placed a circle over the word in question, and placed in the margin the consonants of the word which they proposed to substitute. This marginal reading is called the Q'ri—*i. e.*, "read." It is pronounced with the Massoretic points attached to. but not belonging to the Text. How the K'thibh or word in the Text is to be pronounced is not indicated. The points proper for its pronunciation must be supplied from one's knowledge of the language.

Note that the emended word in the Text, if pronounced with the Massoretic points there attached to it, is usually no part of speech, but a mere mixture of K'thibh and the points of Q'ri.

Note also that as regards pronunciation the distinction between Q'ri and K'thibh may be, 1st, in both consonants and points; 2d, in consonants only; or, 3d, in points only.

§ 73. SOME PRIMITIVE FORMS.

Cf. §§ 6 and 67.

1. וֹם $\left\{ \begin{array}{c} \text{וֹן} \\ \text{ים} \end{array} \right.$ ' $\left\{ \begin{array}{c} \text{יֹן} \\ \text{ם} \end{array} \right.$

2. אַתְּ of אַתְּי (אַתְּי)

3. קְטָל, of קְטַל (see remark below).

4. דְּקִטְלָה of דָּקְטְלַת (קְטַלַת)

5. קְטַלְתְּ of קָטַלְתִּי, cf. 2 above.

6. קְטַלְתֶּם of קְטַלְתּוּם

7. יִקְטֹל of יְקְטֹל ⎫
8. נִקְטַל of נְקְטַל ⎭ chireq auxiliary, § 41.

9. קְטֵל of קַטֵּל

10. הִקְטִיל of הַקְטִיל

11. סוּסָה of סוּסַת (cf. 4 of this table).

Remark on § 73, 3.—In qal preterite, the first radical drops its vowel when it ceases to be pretonic, owing to the addition of a suffix or of a mixed affix (i. e., of an affix consisting of a mixed syllable), cf. §§ 21 and 67.

DEVELOPMENTS.

§ 74. In developing a form proceed from left to right.

(a) In developing a verb follow the analogy of קָטַל so far as to obtain the simplest form of the tense or mode in question—*i. e.*, the 3d sing. masc. (in the imperative, the 2d sing. masc.). To obtain the remaining persons and number, make the proper additions to the form thus obtained— *e. g.*, to develop the hiph. pret. 2d plur. masc. of סָבַב we do not begin by writing down הִקְטַלְתֶּם for guidance, but start with its simplest form—*i. e.*, the 3d sing. masc. הִקְטִיל Following the analogy of this we have הִסְבִּיב Applying the proper principles we obtain הֵסֵב Now adding תֶּם and applying the proper principles we get הֲסִבֹּתֶם

(b) In developing a noun, indicate what is involved, leaving blanks to be filled in reverse order—*e. g.*, let us assume the form כֶּלֶד to be a noun meaning horse, then indicating what according to rules is involved, we have the following to obtain my mares.

1 plur. fem. with light suffix;
2 cst. plur. fem.;

3 abs. plur. fem.;

4. abs. sing. masc.

Then starting with the last (which is given), viz., כָּלָד we fill up the blanks in reverse order— *i. e.*, from below up. The numbers indicate the order of the steps.

1 plur. fem. with light suffix,   כְּלָדֹתַי 4

2 cst. plur. fem.,   .   .   .   כְּלָדֹת 3

3 abs. pl. fem.,   .   .   .   כְּלָדֹת 2

4 abs. sing. masc.,   .   .   .   כָּלָד 1

EXAMPLES IN DEVELOPMENTS.

Nouns.

Assuming כָּלָד to be a noun, meaning horse, develop the following:

§ 75. My horse. This involves the following steps:

1 sing. masc. with light suffix, כְּלָדִי 3. § 53.

2 abs. pl. masc.,   .   .   כְּלָדִים 2. § 47 (*b*)

3 abs. sing. masc ,   .   כָּלָד 1.

§ 76. My horses.

1 pl. masc. with light suffix, כְּלָדִי 3. § 53.

2 abs. pl. masc.,   . .   כְּלָדִים 2. § 47 (b)

3 abs. sing. masc.,   .   כָּלָד 1.

77. Your horse.

1 sing. masc. with grave,   כְּלַדְכֶם 3. § 51 and § 28.

2 cst. sing. masc.,   .   כְּלָד 2. § 49 (a) and (b).

3 abs. sing. masc.,   .   כָּלָד 1.

78. Your horses.

1 pl. masc. with grave suffix,   כְּלָדֶיכֶם 4. § 51.

2 cst. pl. masc., כְּלָדֵי 3. § 41, 1 (a) & § 49 Rem.

       (כְּלָדֵי)   § 49 (b).

3 abs. pl. masc.,   . .   כְּלָדִים 2. § 47 (b)

4 abs. sing. masc.,   . .   כָּלָד 1.

79. My mare.

1 sing. fem. with light suffix, כְּלָדָתִי 4. § 52.*

2 cst. sing. fem.,   .   .   כְּלָדַת 3. § 41, 1 (a)

       (כְּלָדַת)   § 49 (b).

* Tone by § 16, hence kamets by § 10 (a).

3 abs. sing. fem., . . כְּלָדָה 2. § 47 (b).

4 abs. sing. masc., . כְּלָד 1.

§ 80. My mares.

1 pl. fem. with light suffix, כְּלָדֹתָי 4. § 52.

2 cst. pl. fem., כְּלָדֹת 3. § 41, 1 (a) & § 49 Rem.

(כְּלָדֹת) § 49 (b).

3 abs. pl. fem., . . כְּלָדֹת 2. § 47 (b).

4 abs. sing. masc., . . כְּלָד 1.

§ 81. Your mare.

1 sing. fem. with grave suffix, כְּלָדָּתְכֶם 4. § 51
and § 28.

2 cst. sing. fem., . כְּלָדַּת 3. § 41, 1 (a).

(כְּלָדַּת) § 49 (b).

3 abs. sing. fem., . . כְּלָדָה 2. § 47 (b).

4 abs. sing. masc., . כְּלָד 1.

§ 82. Your mares.

1 pl. fem. with grave suffix, כְּלָדֹתֵיכֶם 4. § 51.

2 cst. pl. fem., כְּלָדֹת 3. § 41, 1 (a) & § 49 Rem.

(כְּלָדֹת) § 49 (b).

3 abs. pl. fem., . .. כְּלָדֹת 2. § 47 (b).

4 abs. sing. masc., . כְּלָד 1.

83. My twin horses.

1 dual masc. with light suffix, כְּלָדַי 3. § 54.

2 abs. dual masc., . . כְּלָדַיִם 2. § 47 (b).

3. abs. sing. masc., . . כְּלָד 1.

84. Your twin horses.

1 dual masc. with grave suffix, כְּלָדֵיכֶם 4. § 51.

2 cst. dual masc., כְּלָדֵי 3. § 41, 1 (a) & § 49 Rem.

(כְּלָדֵי) § 49 (b).

3 abs. dual masc., . כְּלָדַיִם 2. § 47 (b).

4 abs. sing. masc., . כְּלָד 1.

85. My twin mares.

1 dual fem. with light suffix, כְּלָדָתִי 4. § 54.

2 abs. dual fem.,   .   כְּלִדָּתַיִם 3. § 41, 1 (*a*).

(כְּלִדָּתָיִם) § 47, Rem. 1 & (*b*),

3 abs. sing. fem. pr. form,   .   כְּלָדַת 2.

(כְּלָדָה) § 47 *b*).

4 abs. sing. masc.,   . . .   כָּלָד 1.

§ 86. Your twin mares.

1 dual fem. with grave suffix, כְּלִדָתֵיכֶם 5. § 51.

2 cst. dual fem.,   . .   כְּלִדָּתֵי 4. § 49 (*b*).

3 abs. dual fem.,   .   כְּלִדָּתַיִם 3. § 41, 1 (*a*).

(כְּלִדָּתָיִם) § 47, Rem. 1 & (*b*) & § 10.

4 abs. sing. fem. pr. form,   .   כְּלָדַת 2.

(כְּלָדָה, § 47 *b*).

5 abs. sing. masc.,   . .   כָּלָד 1.

SEGHOLATES.

Assuming the form כֶּלֶד with primitive vowel pattahh to mean horse, develop the following.

§ 87. My horse.

    1 sing. masc. with light suffix, כְּלִדִי 2. § 46 (*a*)
       & R. 1.
    2 primitive form, . . כַּלְדְּ 1.

§ 88. My horses.

    1 pl. masc. with light suffix, כְּלָדַי 3. § 53.

    2 abs. pl. masc., . . כְּלָדִים 2. § 45.

    3 abs. sing. masc., . . כְּלָד 1.

§ 89. Your horse.

    1 sing. masc. with grave suffix, כַּלְדְּכֶם 2. § 46
       (*a*) & Rem. 1.
    2 primitive form, . . . כַּלְדְּ 1.

§ 90. Your horses.

    1 pl. masc. with grave suffix, כַּלְדֵיכֶם 4. § 51.

    2 cst. pl. masc., (כַּלְדֵי § 49 *b*), כַּלְדֵי 3. § 41,
       1 (*c*), § 46 (*c*), and § 49, Rem.

    3 abs. pl. masc. and pr. form, כְּלָדִים 2. § 45.

                      כַּלְדְּ

    4 abs. sing. masc., . . . כְּלָד 1.

§ 91. My mare.

    1 sing. fem. with light suffix, כַּלְדָּתִי 4. § 52.

    2 cst. sing. fem.,   . .   כַּלְדַּת 3. § 49.

    3 abs. sing. fem., כַּלְדָּה 2. § 46 (*b*) & Rem. 1.

    4 primitive form,   . .   כַּלְדְּ 1.

§ 92. My mares.

    1 pl. fem. with light suffix, כַּלְדֹתַי 4. § 52.

    2 cst. pl. fem., (כַּלְדֹת § 49, *b*), כַּלְדֹת 3. § 41,
      1 (*c*), § 46 (*c*), and § 49, Rem.

    3 abs. pl. fem. and pr. form, כְּלָדֹת 2. § 45. כַּלְדְּ

    4 abs. sing. masc.,   . .   כְּלֶד 1.

§ 93. Your mare.

    1 sing. fem. with grave suffix, כַּלְדַּתְכֶם 4. § 51
      and § 28.

    2 cst. sing. fem.,   . .   כַּלְדַּת 3. § 49.

    3 abs. sing. fem., כַּלְדָּה 2. § 46 (*b*), & Rem. 1.

    4 primitive form,   . . .   כַּלְדְּ 1.

§ 94. Your mares.

   1 pl. fem. with grave suffix, כַּלְדֹתֵיכֶם 4.

   2 cst. pl. fem. (כִּלְדֹת § 49, b) כַּלְדֹת 3. § 41,
      1 (c), § 46 (c), and § 49 Rem.

   3 abs. pl. fem. and pr. form, כַּלְדֹת 2. § 45. כַּלְדָּה

   4 abs. sing. masc.,   .   .   .   כַּלְדָּה 1.

§ 95. My twin horses.

   1 dual masc. with light suffix, כַּלְדַּי 3. § 54.

   2 abs. dual masc., כַּלְדַּיִם 2. § 46 (d) & Rem. 1.

   3 pr. form.,   .   .   .   כַּלְד 1.

§ 96. 1. Your twin horses.

   1 dual masc. with grave suffix, כַּלְדֵיכֶם 4. § 51.

   2 cst. dual masc.,   .   כַּלְדֵי 3. § 49 & 46 (c).

   3 abs. dual masc. and pr. form, כַּלְדַּיִם 2. § 46
      (d) and Rem., כַּלְד

   4 pr. form, ...   כַּלְד 1.

   2. If the absolute dual have pretonic kamets,
as it sometimes has, § 36, the development is as follows:

1 dual masc. with grave suffix, כַּלְדֵיכֶם 4. § 51.

2 cst. dual masc. (כַּלְדֵי § 49 (b), & Rem.) כַּלְדֵי

   3. § 41, 1 (c), § 46 (c), & § 49, Remark.

3 abs. dual masc. and pr. form, כַּלְדַיִם 2. § 45,

כַּלְדְ

4 abs. sing. masc., . . . כָּלְדְ 1.

§ 97. My twin mares.

1 dual fem. with light suffix, כַּלְדָתָי 4. § 54.

2 abs. dual fem., . כַּלְדָתַיִם 3. § 47, Rem. 1.

3 abs. sing. fem. pr. form, כַּלְדַּת 2.

                   (כַּלְדָה § 46, b)

4 pr. form, . . . כָּלְדְ 1.

§ 98. Your twin mares.

1 dual fem. with grave suffix, כַּלְדָתֵיכֶם 5. § 51.

2 dual fem. cst., . . כַּלְדָתֵי 4. § 49 (b).

3 abs. dual. fem., כַּלְדָתַיִם 3. § 47, Rem. 1.

4 abs. sing. fem. pr. form, כַּלְדַּ֫ת 2. (כַּלְדָּ֫ה

§ 46 *b*).

5 pr. form, . . . כַּלְדְּ 1.

§ 99.　To develop כְּלִי֫וֹ from כֹּל

　　The addition וֹ takes tone by § 16.　This would
give כֹּלִי֫וֹ　But the root being כָּלַל, the ל must
take daghesh to represent the second ל　This
would give כֹּלִּי֫וֹ, which by §§ 10 and 33 (*c*) becomes כְּלִי֫וֹ

VERBS.

With suffixes.　See §§ 67 and 74.

§ 100.　To develop קְטָלוֹ֫　From § 73, 3, we have קָטַל֫
Adding הוּ and connecting vowel of pret.,
קְטָלְ֫הוּ　Tone by § 18.　By § 10 we have
קְטָלָ֫הוּ, which by contraction becomes (a + u
= o) קְטָלוֹ֫
　　(*a*). By a like contraction קְטַלְתָּ֫הוּ = קְטַלְתּוֹ֫

Note.—W, y, and sometimes h coming between two vowels are sometimes lost in the
vowel stream surrounding them.

§ 101. To develop קָטְלָהּ׃

From § 73, 3, we have קְטַל Adding הָ and connecting vowel of pret. קְטַלָה Tone by § 18. By § 10 we have קְטָלָה To avoid the recurrence of so many successive "a" sounds, the last one is dropped, and a mappik is placed in ה to indicate its character as a consonant קְטָלָהּ

§ 102. To develop קְטַלְתּוּ From § 73, 3, we have קְטַל Adding ת - the old feminine termination, קְטָלַת § 73, 4. Tone by § 17 (a). Adding הוּ and accenting by § 18, lengthening vowel of ט by § 10, קְטָלַתְהוּ which by contraction become קְטָלַתּוּ

(a) In like manner קְטָלַתְהָ contracts into קְטָלַתָּה

§ 103. To develop קְטַלְתֶּם By § 73, 3, we have קְטַל which by the addition of the old feminine ending ת - becomes קְטָלַת § 73, 4. On adding the suffix ם the question arises whether to use ă or ā as the union vowel. Now, in either case we should have an asyllabic addition to a verb as suffix, which by § 17 (b) draws the tone forward (only) one syllable, and, therefore, not far enough to reach the union vowel. The latter, therefore, by § 10, cannot be ā. Hence we have קְטַלְתֶּם which by § 10 (*b*) becomes קְטָלְתֶּם

§ 104. To develop קְטַלְתִּינִי By § 73, 5, we have קְטַלְתִּי which by the addition of נִי becomes קְטַלְתִּינִי

§ 105. To develop קְטַלְתּוּנִי By § 73, 6, we have קְטַלְתּוּם Adding נִי and rejecting ם for euphony, קְטַלְתּוּנִי

§ 106. To develop קָטְלִי Starting with קְטֹל (inf. cst.), and adding יָ. we have, after the analogy of § 66, קְטֹלִי which by § 41, 1 (*c*), on account of the dropped "o" sound, becomes קָטְלִי, the first syllable being intermediate, §§ 2 and 3.

VERBS PE GUTTURAL.

§ 107. To develop עֲמְדִי qal imperative. After the analogy of קְטֹל we should have עֲמֹד which

by § 39 becomes עֲמֹד. Adding י, we have by
§ 66 עֲמָדִי which by § 41, 1 (b) becomes עָמְדִי,
the first syllable being intermediate.

§ 108. To develop יַעֲמְדוּ. After the analogy of יִקְטֹל
§ 73, 7, we should have יַעֲמֹד, which by § 39
becomes יַעֲמֹד, which by § 41, 2, becomes
יַעֲמֹד, methegh by § 25 (c). The first syllable
is intermediate. Adding וּ, by § 66 we have
יַעֲמְדוּ, which by § 41, 3 (b), becomes יַעַמְדוּ.
The first two syllables are intermediate.

§ 109. To develop נֶעֶמְדוּ. After the analogy of נִקְטֹל
§ 73, 8, we should have נֶעֱמֹד which, by § 39
and § 41, 2, would become נֶעֱמֹד. But as the recurrence of so many successive "a" sounds is
avoided when they are not *essential*, ֱ is used,
being the compound sh'va next akin to ֶ. We
thus have נֶעֱמֹד. Adding וּ, by § 66 we have
נֶעֱמְדוּ, which, by § 41, 3 (b), becomes נֶעֶמְדוּ.
(a) In like manner is developed יֶחֱזְקוּ.

§ 110. To develop יֵעָמֵד. After the analogy of יִקָּטֵל
we should expect יֵעָמֵד. But the guttural not

being able to take daghesh, and the preceding vowel being lengthened in consequence, the latter becomes tsere by § 33 (*a*).

§ 111. To develop הֶעֱמִיד. After the analogy of הִקְטִיל we should have הֶעֲמִיד. By § 39, ע should take a compound sh'va. But as this vowel should be homogeneous with that of the preformative, and as there is no such compound sh'va as chateph-chireq, the preformative takes the vowel next akin to chireq, viz., seghol, which has a homogeneous compound sh'va. We thus get הֶעֱמִיד.

§ 112. To develop הָעֶמְדָה. After the analogy of הָקְטֵל we should have הָעֳמִד. By § 39, the sh'va conforming with the short "o" sound, we have הָעֳמִד. Adding ה ָ we have, by § 66, הָעֳמְדָה, which by § 41, 3 (*b*) becomes הָעֶמְדָה.

VERBS AYIN GUTTURAL.

§ 113. To develop שָׁחַטְתִּי. Following the analogy of קָטֵל in the pointing of its first radical, but § 56 in the vowel of its second radical, we have שָׁחַט. Adding יֹ and applying § 66, we have שָׁחַטְיֹ, which by § 41, 2, becomes שַׁחַטְיֹ.

§ 114. To develop בֵּרֶךְ. By analogy of קְטֵל we should have בִּרֵךְ. But, owing to the inability of ר to take daghesh forte, chireq is lengthened, and by § 33 (a) becomes tsere, thus giving בֵּרֵךְ.

§ 115. To develop בֹּרַךְ. After the analogy of קְטֵל we should have בֻּרַךְ. But, owing to the inability of ר to take daghesh forte, qibbuts is lengthened, and by § 33 (a) becomes cholem, thus giving בֹּרַךְ.

VERBS PE NUN.

§ 116. To develop הִגִּישׁ. After the analogy of הִקְטִיל we should have הִנְגִּישׁ, which by § 58 (a) becomes הִגִּישׁ.

§ 117. To develop הֻגַּשׁ. By analogy of הָקְטַל we should have הֻנְגַּשׁ, which by § 58 (a) becomes הֻגַּשׁ, and this by § 33 (c) becomes הֻגַּשׁ.

VERBS AYIN DOUBLED.

§ 118. To develop סַבּוֹתֶם. By analogy of קָטֵל (§ 73, 3), we should have סָבַב, which by § 59 becomes

סַב. Adding תֶם, and ו by § 62, and inserting daghesh on account of the omitted בּ, we have סַבּוֹתֶם.

§ 119. To develop תְּסֻבֶּינָה. By analogy of יִקְטֹל (§ 73, 7), we should have יִסְבֹב, which by § 59 becomes יִסֹב, and this יָסֹב § 40. Attaching the proper prefix and affix, we have תָּסֹבְנָה, which by § 62 becomes תְּסֻבֶּינָה (tone by § 18, and daghesh on account of the omitted בּ). Applying § 33 (c), and dropping pretonic qamets, because תּ is no longer immediately before the tone (cf. also § 21), we have תְּסֻבֶּינָה.

§ 120. To develop נְסַבּוֹת. After the analogy of נִקְטֹל (§ 73, 8), we should have נִסְבַב, which by § 59 becomes נִסַב, and this נָסַב § 40. Adding תּ, and cholem by § 62, we have נָסַבּוֹת (tone by § 18, and daghesh to compensate for the omitted בּ). Dropping pretonic qamets because נ is no longer immediately before the tone (cf. also § 21), we have נְסַבּוֹת.

§ 121. To develop הֲסֻבּוֹת. By analogy of הִקְטִיל

we should have הֶחְסָבִיב, which by § 59 becomes הֶסִיב, and this by § 33 (b) (ב being doubled here) becomes הֶסֵּב, which by § 10 becomes הֵסֵב. Adding תָ, applying § 62, accenting, and applying § 33 (c) and § 21, we have הֲסִבּוֹתָ.

§ 122. To develop תְסֻבֶּינָה. After the analogy of יַקְטִיל we should have יַסְבִּיב, which by § 59 becomes יַסִיב, and this by § 33 (b) (ב being doubled here) becomes יַסֵּב, which by § 10 becomes יָסֵב. Attaching the proper prefix and affix, we have תָּסֻבֶּנָה which by § 62 becomes תָסֻבֶּינָה (tone by § 18 and daghesh on account of omitted ב). Applying 33 (c), and dropping pretonic qamets, because ה is no longer immediately before the tone (cf. also § 21), we have תְסֻבֶּינָה.

§ 123. To develop יְסֻבֵּנִי. § 122 shows us how to obtain יָסֵב. Adding the suffix, and the connecting vowel of the future, we have יָסֻבֵנִי (tone by § 18). Inserting daghesh on account of the omitted ב, applying § 33 (c), and dropping qamets, because no longer immediately before the tone (cf. also § 21), we have יְסֻבֵּנִי.

124. To develop הוּסַב. By analogy of הָקְטֵל we should have הָסְבַּב, which by § 59 becomes הָסַב, and this by § 10 becomes הוּסַב.

VERBS AYIN VAV.

125. To develop וַיָּקֶם. Adding י to the qal inf. קוּם by § 55 (a), we have יְקוּם, which by § 40 becomes יָקוּם (cf. also 61). Vav conversive requires the jussive form, and this by § 65, 1, is יָקֻם. Prefixing the vav, accenting by § 14, and applying § 10, we have וַיָּקֶם.

126. To develop קְמָנָה. § 125 gives the development of the qal fut., from which, by dropping the prefix (§ 55, a), we get the imperative קוּם. Adding נָה accenting by § 18, and applying § 33 (b), we get קְמָנָה.

127. To develop נָקוֹם. After the analogy of נִקְטֵל § 73, 8, we should have נִקְוַם, which by § 60 becomes נִקֻּום, and then by § 60 (b) נִקוֹם, and this by § 40 נָקוֹם.

128. To develop הֵקִים. After the analogy of הִקְטִיל we should have הִקְוִים, which by § 60 becomes

40

הֲקִיוֹם, and then by § 60 (a) הֲקִים, and this by § 10 הֲקִים.

§ 129. To develop וַיָּקֶם. Adding ו to the hiph. inf. הָקִים by § 55 (a) we have יְהָקִים, and by contraction, after the analogy of the excluded article, יָקִים. Vav conversive requires the jussive form, and this by § 65, 1, is יָקֶם. Prefixing the vav, accenting by § 14, and applying § 10, we get וַיָּקֶם.

§ 130. To develop הוּקַם. After the analogy of הָקְטַל we should have הָקֻוֹם, and then by § 60 הָקֻוֹם which by § 60 (a) becomes הָקַם, and then by § 10 הוּקַם.

VERBS PE YODH PR. PE VAV. (See § 63.)

§ 131. To develop נוֹשַׁב. After the analogy of נִקְטַל (§ 73, 8) we should have נִוְשַׁב. By § 41, 1 (a) we should expect נוְשַׁב. But as i and u (the u being represented here by the semi-vowel vav) cannot combine (§ 33), and i is not here an essential or characteristic vowel, but only an accidental or auxiliary vowel, while pattach, the next shortest vowel, can combine with u, there-

fore pattach is substituted as the auxiliary vowel,
thus giving נַוְשַׁב, and by combination נוֹשַׁב.

132. To develop הוֹשִׁיב (preterite). By analogy of
הִקְטִיל we should have הִוְשִׁיב. But as i and u
cannot combine (§ 33), we resort to the primitive pointing הַוְשִׁיב (§ 73, 10), which by combination gives הוֹשִׁיב.

133. To develop הוּשַׁב. By analogy of הָקְטַל we
should have הָוְשַׁב. By the quiescence of vav
in the " o " sound, we have הָוֹשַׁב, which by
§ 10 becomes הוּשַׁב.

VERBS PROPERLY PE YODH.

134. To develop יֵיטִיב. After the analogy of יַקְטִיל
we should have יֵיְטִיב, which by combination
(§ 33) gives יֵיטִיב, the second yodh in this
last word being merely a quiescent.

VERBS LAMEDH HE.

135. To develop גָּלוֹ. By analogy of קָטַל we should
have גָּלִי with its original yodh. Adding ן, and
applying § 66 we have גָּלִיןֻ (tone by § 17 [a], § 8

[*a*] and [*b*] and § 9 [*a*]), which by § 64, 2 becomes
גְּלֽוּ׃

Remark. Note that if the word were milel it would be the same part of the root גּוּל or גִּיל. The singular being גָּל the addition of וּ disturbs no vowel, but leaves the tone were it was, thus גָּלֽוּ׃

§ 136. To develop יִגְל. After the analogy of יִקְטֹל, except that these verbs are properly middle *a* in the future, we have יִגְלִי, which by combination, § 33 (*i* being represented here by the semi-vowel yodh), becomes יִגְלֶה, ה being merely a quiescent here. Apocopating gives us יִגְל which by § 33 (*b*) may become יִגֶל. Taking a helping vowel it becomes יִגֶל, tone by § 9 (*b*) and § 15.

Remark. By the same combination the noun שָׂדֵי becomes שָׂדֶה.

§ 137. To develop יִהְי. § 136 shows us the development so far as יִהְיֶה. Apocopating gives יִהְי. Final yodh, being more difficult to pronounce without a vowel than initial yodh, attracts and quiesces in

the homogeneous vowel chireq, which the first yodh
surrenders.   We thus get יִרְֽהִי.

§ 138. To develop יִשְׁתַּֽחֲוּ, hithpalel of שָׁחָה, in which
conjugation the last radical is doubled, thus—
יִתְקַטְלֵל, instead of the middle as in יִתְקַטֵּל,
the hithpael. After   the   analogy,   then,   of
יִתְקַטְלֵל (except that the guttural takes, as
usual, compound sh'va, and that the last radical
vav conforms to the laws of lamedh he verbs,
and so the second vav here disappears) we have
יִתְשַׁחֲוֶה, which by metathesis becomes יִשְׁתַּחֲוֶה.
Apocopating we have יִשְׁתַּֽחְוְ. In order to aid
in the pronunciation, vav is here softened into its
homogeneous vowel u (shureq), which, being here
a helping vowel, does not take tone, § 9 (b). We
thus get יִשְׁתַּֽחוּ